Via Ben venuto Cellini 14

ROADS Publishing
149 Lower Baggot Street
Dublin 2
Ireland

www.roads.co

First published 2017

1

Milan: The Considered Guide

Text copyright
© ROADS Publishing

Design and layout copyright
© ROADS Publishing

Photographs
© The copyright holders, pg. 140

Cover Image
© Getty Images/Westend61/Carmen Steiner

All of the businesses herein were chosen at the discretion of the publishers.
No payments or incentives were offered or received to ensure inclusion.

Art direction by
Alessio Avventuroso

Designed by
Agenzia del Contemporaneo

Printed in Italy
Grafiche Damiani – Faenza Group SpA

978-1-909399-96-9

Milan

The Considered Guide

Growing up, travel was a major part of my life. It was and remains an integral source of education and inspiration. When I travel, I actively search out the most interesting and innovative places. As a rule, I ask my friends and contacts in each city for a list of their favourite places. I then keep and share with others my lists of places both recommended and those I discovered myself. Therefore, I decided to create the kind of travel guide that I myself would find useful: a carefully edited selection of the best places in a city – a book that is practical, beautiful, and, crucially, trustworthy.

The Considered Guide reflects the desires of the discerning traveller who cares deeply about how they spend their valuable time and money, and who appreciates impeccable service, beautiful design and attention to detail at every price level.

I am proud to say that I visited each and every place in this guide, and can vouch for the quality of each of them as personal recommendations.

Danielle Ryan
Founder of ROADS

Introduction

Milan means business. As the economic capital of Italy, it has a wealth of thriving industrial sectors, including automobiles, machinery, textile and chemical production, a rapidly developing communications and media network, and, of course, it is one of the world's top fashion cities.

Its reputation as a centre of industry means that it is often overlooked in a country with an embarrassment of riches to offer tourists, but Milan is an inspiring place to visit; on every level it is a hive of creative activity – in culture, design, art, gastronomy, and more.

Milan covers approximately 182 square kilometres in the Po Basin of Lombardy, bordered by the Alps to the north and the River Po to the south. The city dates from around 400 BC, and has experienced consistent change since then. It has been governed by the Celts, Romans, Goths, Spaniards and Austrians, and all this before the unification of Italy in the nineteenth century and the chaos of the twentieth century, which saw the rise of fascism and the devastation of World War II, during which Milan was to suffer terribly. Some of the city's most important cultural edifices were destroyed or seriously damaged, including the Cathedral, La Scala and the Galleria Vittorio Emanuele II, in a campaign that left some 400,000 people homeless. Today, the city is home to 1.3 million people and thankfully many of its landmarks have been lovingly restored to their former glories.

While it is true that Milan has a striking sense of purpose, the city also knows how to enjoy itself. The restaurant scene is impeccable at all price points, with a galaxy of Michelin-starred restaurants and a host of regional specialities commonly available, such as risotto alla Milanese, osso buco, and panettone. There are lots of interesting things happening in terms of nightlife, with young entrepreneurs experimenting with distillation, creative spaces and artistic collaborations. For something more traditional, a performance at La Scala never fails to impress, and the gilded Fondazione Prada and cutting-edge HangarBicocca have been welcome additions to the visual arts scene.

In Milan, there is a pervasive contrast of tradition and innovation. With an eye to the dedication and craftsmanship of the past, the city is always looking forward. These pleasing contrasts are everywhere, from the largest monument to the smallest detail. Just compare the Duomo and il Bosco Verticale: the former is a Gothic masterpiece, begun in the 1380s, the latter is a modern architectural marvel, inaugurated in 2014, in which two towers play host to thousands of plants and trees. Or walk the short stroll from Galleria Vittorio Emanuele II (1877), the oldest luxury shopping centre in the world, to the crisp, modern Il Rinascente, where Cavalli, Pucci, Versace, and all the modern Italian masters of fashion stand side by side.

With its sterling heritage in textile production and design, it is unsurprising that Milan came to be known as one of the world's fashion capitals. Here, the quality of materials is king, and most Italian fashion houses, no matter their origins, have ateliers in the city. Every spring and autumn, thousands of beautiful people flock to Milan Fashion Week and many of the city's landmarks become stunning temporary catwalks. The city pulsates during fashion weeks, but it should come as no surprise that demand and prices rise accordingly.

Rather than the designated title of Italy's 'Second City', the people of Milan prefer to think of their home as the 'Moral City' – they take pride in their strong work ethic and in always striving for improvement. They work hard and they play hard, and as a result every taste is catered for in style, making Milan the perfect place for an eclectic, chic and cultured city break.

Visitors to Milan are twice blessed in terms of transportation: firstly, the historic centre of the city, where the majority of attractions are situated, is compact, flat and easy to navigate on foot; secondly, Milan has an efficient and extremely good-value public transport system. Azienda Trasporti Milanesi (ATM) operates the underground and overground transport network, comprising a metro rail system, buses and trams. A single ticket (€1.50, from stations, kiosks or tabacchi) offers ninety minutes of unlimited travel across these networks – just remember to stamp your ticket every time you change. When you get your bearings, you might like to hire a city bike for the afternoon, take a ride on a historic trolley bus, or take a day trip on the train to one of Milan's charming satellite towns.

Getting around

From the airport

Milan has three airports: Malpensa, Linate, and Orio al Serio/Bergamo. Travellers to Malpensa have the choice of two train services, one to Cadorna station and the other to Garibaldi and Milano Centrale (both €13 one way), and three shuttle bus services (€8-€10). A taxi to the city centre should cost around €95. From Linate, you can take an ATM city bus to the San Babila metro stop near the Duomo, or travel by coach to Centrale. From Orio al Serio/Bergamo, there are three coach services. Tickets cost approximately €5 one way, and the journey is 60-90 minutes, depending on traffic.

Taxis

Despite the great public transport links, and the heavy traffic, taxis remain hugely popular in Milan. Hailing a taxi is difficult, so look for a taxi rank, or use Uber. The cost of taxi journeys is determined by meter, and starting prices vary according to the time of day (from approximately €3.50 during the day to €6.50 at night). While some taxis can accept cards, it is better to be prepared and carry cash.

Underground
atm.it/en

Milan has four underground lines (a fifth is currently under construction) and between them most of the city is catered for. Trains operate from around 6am to 1am, depending on the line. Metro stations are indicated by red-and-white 'M' lampposts, and the maps, with their four brightly coloured lines, are easy to navigate. Hold on to your ticket, and always validate on new journeys.

Buses and Trams
atm.it/en

Between buses, trams and trolleys, ATM operates more than eighty lines across the city. Depending on the route, buses run from 5.30am to 1.30am, and there are night-bus routes at the weekends (check the website for current listings). The 94 bus is particularly convenient

for tourists, as it circles the city centre, close to all most popular tourist destinations. Some of the tram lines still run 1920s tram cars; this is an experience in itself, but not the best choice if you're in a hurry. With buses and trams, don't forget to validate your ticket upon embarking.

Bike Sharing
bikemi.com

BikeMi is Milan's city-bike scheme that allows tourists and locals to pick up and drop off a bicycle at a wide range of locations. New stops are added frequently, but the tourist centre is already well catered for. The

first 30 minutes are free, a day costs €4.50, and a week's rental is €9.

Trains
italiarail.com

Milan is ideally located for reaching other towns by train. Commuter trains link the city to Bergamo, Verona, Vicenza, to the mountains, to Lake Como and Lake Maggiore, and much more. Onward journeys to larger cities are very straightforward. Milan's largest train station, Centrale, also has a left luggage service that operates from 6am to midnight daily.

Hotels

3Rooms
10 Corso
Como

€€€€

As the name suggest, there are only three rooms in this hotel, each with its own character and colour palette, and with generous lounge areas and bathrooms. The rooms are located above the iconic 10 Corso Como store, on what is arguably Milan's trendiest street. The boutique on the two lower floors of the building is beloved among design enthusiasts, and the emphasis on design carries through to the accommodation, where the furniture and furnishings are the work of big names in Italian and international design, including Eero Saarinen and Arne Jacobsen. The rooms are serviced by the restaurant downstairs and breakfast can be eaten in the building's beautiful green courtyard.

—

Corso Como 10, 20154 Milano
3rooms-10corsocomo.com
+39 02 626163

Armani Hotel

With every minute detail having been overseen by
Giorgio Armani himself, the Armani Hotel offers the most
luxurious experience imaginable. Centrally located, in the
heart of the exclusive fashion district, the focus is on the
Armani aesthetic: minimal and sophisticated, with sandy
beige hues offset by black marble and mother of pearl.
This attention to detail extends to service; on check-in,
every guest is assigned a 'Lifestyle Manager', and each
of the ninety-five rooms has an iPod-controlled sound
system. Make the most of the experience and enjoy the
spa's relaxation pool, the Bamboo Bar and the Michelin-
starred restaurant.

€€€€+

—

Via Alessandro Manzoni 31, 20121 Milano
milan.armanihotels.com
+39 02 8883 8888

Madama Hostel

€

Madama Hostel was once home to a police station. The current ambience couldn't be more different, however; there's a friendly community atmosphere, with art hanging on the walls and rough-and-ready recycled furniture. Guests can choose from female-only or mixed dorms, or double rooms, and all have air conditioning and private toilets. Located close to the Fondazione Prada (pg. 52), you can rent a bike here for a few euro, so it's a great hub for sightseeing. The quirky ground-floor bar and bistro is an excellent place to begin a night out and to meet other visitors to Milan. Room prices include a welcome drink and breakfast.

—

Via Benaco 1, 2013 Milano
madamahostel.com
+39 02 36727370

Palazzo Segreti

Palazzo Segreti is a carefully restored nineteenth-century palace with uber modern, subdued interiors. It houses eighteen individually designed contemporary bedrooms and suites, and a very chic lounge bar. The avant-garde design features modern artwork (it changes every month) hanging on bare concrete walls, accented with intense bursts of colour. Located in the heart of Milan, and boasting excellent customer service, Palazzo Segreti is a great choice for those seeking to experience the famed Milanese high-end aesthetic.

€€€

—

Via San Tomaso 8, 20121 Milano
palazzosegreti.com
+39 02 49529250

Room Mate Giulia

Room Mate Giulia is a hotel with a big personality. The interior of the Milan incarnation is the handiwork of Spanish designer and architect Patricia Urquiola. The colour palette is bright and bold, and incorporates elements of the surrounding urban fabric: the lobby features the same pink marble as the Duomo and terracotta bricks that are typical of Milan. The hotel has eighty-five rooms, a small fitness room, and it couldn't be more central, located as it is beside the Duomo and Galleria Vittorio Emanuelle II.

€€€

—

Via Silvio Pellico 4, 20121 Milano
room-matehotels.com/en/giulia
+39 02 80888900

Senato
Hotel
Milano

€€€

Upon entering the Senato Hotel, you are greeted by a monochrome lobby and an interior courtyard that immediately set the tone for the striking aesthetic throughout. The interiors of the hotel, a rich art deco blend of black, white and gold, are truly special, and infuse the Senato with an easy elegance. The bedrooms are equally attractive, with parquet wooden floors and marble-tiled bathrooms. The hotel is operated by the same family that has owned this building for generations, and this is reflected in the friendly and personal service. Don't miss the café in the patio area and the solarium on the rooftop.

—

Via Senato 22, 20121 Milano
senatohotelmilano.it
+39 02 781236

Straf Hotel

The Italian architect and designer Vincenzo De Cotiis is behind this sophisticated four-star hotel. The edgy deconstructivist aesthetic makes use of industrial features such as brass, iron, oxidised copper, bare cement floors, and scratched and worn mirrors to create the look. Some of the rooms offer terraces with great city views. Located on a side street, a stone's throw from the Duomo, Straf provides attentive and personal service, and despite its austere industrialism, there are welcome touches of luxury such as wellness rooms and a fitness centre. The slick bar frequently hosts international DJs.

€€€

—

Via San Raffaele 3, 20121 Milano
straf.it
+39 02 805081

The Yard Hotel

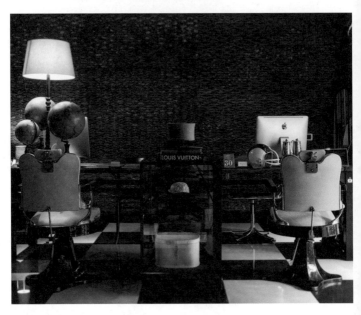

The Yard Hotel has a vintage sports theme, with items such as antique skis, hat boxes, riding boots and bowling balls at every turn. The concept continues to the bedrooms, which are adorned with antique writing desks and cocktail cabinets. Each suite has a different sporting theme: 'Cambridge', for example, is dedicated to the sport of rowing. The boutique hotel is located by the Darsena promenade in the popular Navigli district, and the Milanese come here to enjoy the warm old-timey atmosphere and to sample the creative cocktails from the Doping Club bar.

€€

—

Piazza Maggio 8, 20123 Milano
theyardmilano.com
+39 02 89415901

Shops

10 Corso Como

10 Corso Como is heaven for style lovers. Situated around a beautiful leafy courtyard off the Corso Como, the building houses a chic shopping and dining complex with everything a design enthusiast could wish for, including high-end innovative clothes, books, jewellery, art and music. The careful process of selection has won 10 Corso Como a dedicated following: founded in 1990 by gallerist and publisher Carla Sozzani, it has since opened a number of international branches, including one in Tokyo and one in Shanghai. After some shopping, cool down with an aperitivo in the airy courtyard.

—

Corso Como 10, 20154 Milano
10corsocomo.com
+39 02 29002674

Antonia

Located in the heart of the Brera district and founded by fashion guru Antonia Giancinti in 1999, Antonia boasts an incredible selection of fashion labels. It began life as a women's accessories shop, then it opened a nearby menswear branch, and finally in 2013 the two stores came together in the seventeenth-century Palazzo Cagnola. In a space masterfully renovated by Vicenzo De Cotiis, the beautiful pieces shine against a backdrop of worn and exposed walls with marble and bronze-framed furnishings.

—

Via Cusani 5, 20121 Milano
antonia.it
+39 02 86998340

Biffi

The well-known and ultra-chic Biffi boutique carries an expertly edited selection of the most creative luxury brands in both mens- and womenswear. Established brands such as Dior and Fendi sit comfortably next to the work of up-and-coming designers, as they have quality and innovation in common. Indeed, Biffi is known for having been an early supporter of many modern-day fashion powerhouses (including Kenzo). The large windows flood the space with light and the staff are friendly and savvy, making the shopping experience at Biffi a delight.

—

Corso Genova 6, 20123 Milano
biffi.com
+39 02 83116052

Eataly

The multistorey high-end food emporium Eataly aims to address all your gastronomic needs in one place. Along with Italian delicacies, with locally sourced wine, cheeses, meats and pasta, it houses a number of small food stalls and restaurants, some bars and a renowned cooking school. It also sells kitchen equipment, cookbooks, and artisan foods. An absolute must if you are interested in Italian cuisine.

—

Piazza Venticinque Aprile 10, 20121 Milano
eataly.net
+39 02 49497301

Excelsior Milano

Luxury department store Excelsior is an important destination for the fashion-forward visitor to Milan. Situated in the bustling Duomo area, the seven-storey retail space has an extremely contemporary design, courtesy of Jean Nouvel and Vincenzo De Cotiis, with edgy video installations both inside and outside the building. Inside, you will find the best in clothes, stationery, jewellery and food (concessions include Tiffany & Co. and Ladurée) and exclusive brands such as Balmain, Acne, Valentino, Rick Owens, Christian Louboutin and Missoni.

—

Galleria del Corso 4, 20122 Milano
excelsiormilano.com
+39 02 76307301

Frip

Frip opened as a vintage store in 1994, but by 1998 husband-and-wife team Marcello and Anna Stener had transformed it into Milan's first concept store, and it has been a trailblazer ever since. Located in front of the ancient San Lorenzo columns, inside, Frip is a tiny, minimalist, Scandinavian-inspired space, displaying a carefully selected range of fashion, music and magazines that instils confidence in the quality of each piece. Frip was the first store to bring influential brands such as Acne and Henrik Vibskov to Milan, and it remains consistently ahead of the curve, with up-and-coming brands for men and women. A branch for extremely fashion-forward children, called Frippino, was opened by Anna and Marcello in 2005.

—

Corso di Porta Ticinese 16, 20123 Milano
@frip.it
+39 02 8321360

La Rinascente

La Rinascente is Italy's most esteemed department store group, with eleven branches throughout the country. The flagship and jewel in the company's crown is this stunning building overlooking the Piazza Duomo. In 2016 it was named 'Best Department Store in the World' and it is not difficult to see why, considering the unparalleled location, the beautiful building, and eight sleek storeys of contemporary fashion, homewares, accessories, beauty products and food. Work your way up from the basement Design Store, where over two hundred brands showcase innovative homewares, through the beauty and apparel levels, to the stunning food hall on the top floor, where there are multiple refreshment offerings and breathtaking views along the spires of the Duomo.

—

Piazza Duomo, 20121 Milano
rinascente.it
+39 02 88521

Nilufar

Nilufar is a remarkable furniture gallery that was established in 1979 by Nina Yashar, who was at that time in the business of sourcing exquisite Persian, Chinese, Indian and Tibetan carpets. The company's scope broadened to include furniture and art pieces, and today Yashar is roundly considered to be Milan's most influential design dealer. Nilufar has been in its current home since 1989, where it quickly became the go-to venue for lovers of historical and contemporary furniture pieces. As its popularity grew, the small gallery space could not meet demand, and so the 1,500 square metre Nilufar Depot opened its doors, and it is here that you can really immerse yourself in the scope of these incredible pieces of furniture, each a work of art in its own right.

Vida della Spiga 32, 20121 Milano; Nilufar Depot Viale Vincenzo Lancetti 34, 20158 Milano
nilufar.com
+39 02 780193; +39 02 36590800

Peck

Peck is a high-end culinary emporium that offers the ultimate gastronomic shopping experience. It prides itself on the quality and provenance of its meats and cheeses, and has an amazing selection of wine, teas and coffees, and artisanal chocolates. The Peck team is made up of people who really know their food and love to speak about it, and the show kitchen puts the mastery of accomplished pasta chefs on display. With the addition of a café and a wine-tasting bar, it is well worth spending a few hours here. You will be spoilt for choice, but don't forget to check out the patisserie.

—

Via Spadari 9, 20123 Milano
peck.it
+39 02 8023161

Spazio Rossana Orlandi

Much like its proprietor, Spazio Rossana Orlandi is difficult to define. Situated in a former tie factory in the Corso Magenta district, it is part design showroom, part art gallery, part creative meeting place, and it is wholly absorbing. Rossana Orlandi began as a fashion designer before becoming drawn to textiles and product design. Over time she has become a *bona fide* tastemaker and this space showcases her pick of the best of contemporary design, with the very top names in the industry displayed next to emerging talents. Spazio Rossana Orlandi is open Monday to Friday, 10.30am to 7.30pm; browse the fascinating pieces then head to the associated restaurant for something to eat surrounded by more of Orlandi's collection.

—

Via Matteo Bandello 14/16, 20123 Milano
rossanaorlandi.com
+39 02 4674471

Wait and See ✳

Wait and See is a concept store with a unique vision and a
refreshing sense of fun. Located in Milan's historic city centre,
the store is an expression of the philosophies of founder Uberta
Zambeletti. With a diverse background in fashion, interior design,
and art direction for some of Italy's top brands, Zambeletti
wanted to design a relaxed retail environment that would create
wonder and appreciation of all things beautiful, and that would not
subscribe to preconceived notions of luxury (prices start at just €1).
Everything in store has been carefully chosen to enhance the mood;
customers are invited to enjoy a coffee as they browse the designer
womenswear, accessories, stationery, homewares, and a great
selection of vintage items.

—

Via Santa Marta 14, 20123 Milano
waitandsee.it
+39 02 72080195

What
to See

Fondazione
Prada

Led by famed architect Rem Koolhaas, Fondazione Prada's Milan home is more than an art gallery – it's a cultural hub. In 2011, the compound, a former distillery, was converted into a stylish, contemporary complex, which includes the 'Haunted House', clad in 24-carat gold leaf, and a bar designed by Wes Anderson (pg. 89). The Prada Collection comprises a wealth of twentieth- and twenty-first-century works, and there are regular events relating to art, fashion, design, architecture, philosophy, science, and cinema. Since 1993, Miuccia Prada's non-profit foundation has organised more than one hundred projects with artists including Louise Bourgeois, Carsten Höller, Anish Kapoor, and John Baldessari. Admission is €10 and the complex is open from 10am to 7pm (8pm on Friday and Saturday). Closed Tuesday.

—

Largo Isarco 2, 20139 Milano
fondazioneprada.org
+39 02 56662611

The Last Supper

Leonardo da Vinci's 'Last Supper' is unquestionably one of the world's most important works of art. Painted between 1494 and 1498, the fresco has survived a number of challenges brought about by da Vinci's medium and method, but thanks to several restoration projects it is still on view in the Convent of Santa Maria delle Grazie. In order to limit further deterioration of the work, only twenty-five visitors are permitted in the room at once, and viewings are limited to fifteen minutes. Advance booking is essential, and tickets frequently sell out three months in advance, but if you have the opportunity, do not miss the chance to marvel at one of art's great masterpieces. Modest attire is expected.

—

Piazza di Santa Marie delle Grazie, 20123 Milano
legraziemilano.it
+39 02 4676111

Navigli

Situated in the south-west of the city, this area got its name from the canals (*navigli*) that used to connect Milan with the rivers and lakes in the region. The neighbourhood is bound by Naviglio Grande and Naviglio Pavese, and it has a youthful, artistic vibe. Take the metro green line to Porto Genova, enjoy a walk along the canal, visit the little art galleries, then stop for an aperitivo and watch the crowds swell with revellers in their twenties and thirties who flock here to enjoy the abundance of cafés, bars and clubs. Visitors to Navigli are spoilt for choice, but we recommend Carlo e Camilla (pg. 65), Drogheria (pg. 73), Mag Cafè (pg. 110), and the Botanical Club (pg. 104).

—

Triennale Design Museum

Since the mid-twentieth century, Italy, and Milan in particular, has been a world leader in contemporary design. The Triennale houses a vast collection of iconic works, which it displays alongside temporary exhibitions on fashion, furniture, art, and architecture. This is a dynamic, engaging museum, with plenty to entertain adults and children, in an excellent location along the perimeter of the scenic Parco Sempione (pg. 118). The building, which was constructed in 1933 by Giovanni Muzio for an international exhibition of decorative arts, also houses a library, a DesignCafé, serving the finest Italian coffees, and the Teatro dell'Arte, an experimental space that promotes innovation in artistic expression in fields such as performance and sonic art.

—

Viale Emilio Alemagna 6, 20121 Milano
triennale.org
+39 02 724341

Villa Necchi

Villa Necchi is a splendid piece of art and architecture: built between 1932 and 1935, it was the home of the noble Angelo Campiglio and his family. Now, after extensive restoration, it is a grand escape from the noise of the city. Behind the stone walls there is a wonderful garden with gorgeous magnolia trees, Italy's first outdoor heated swimming pool, and, of course, the villa itself, full of the original furniture of the Campiglio family. If you are into architecture, it is worth checking out the House Museums of Milan Tour, which links Villa Necchi with other three important mansions in the city centre: Poldi Pezzoli Museum, Bagatti Valsecchi Museum, and the Boschi Di Stefano House.

—

Via Mozart 12, 20122 Milano
visitfai.it
+39 02 76340121

Restau-
rants

A Casa Eatery
Alice
Bacaro del Sambuco
Carlo e Camilla in Segheria
Ceresio 7
Giacomo

L'Arabesque
Larte
Drogheria Milanese
Olmetto
Pacifico
Risoelatte

A Santa Lucia
T'a Milano
The Small
Antica Trattoria della Pesa
Vasiliki Kouzina
Zazà Ramen

A Casa Eatery

A Casa Eatery is the perfect name for this special Milanese restaurant; situated off the main thoroughfares, there is the immediate sense that you are walking into a 1960s family home. The décor is eclectic but uncluttered, and tables are widely spaced, creating a sense of intimate privacy. The friendly and knowledgeable staff add to the relaxed ambience, serving refined Neopolitan dishes that are full of flavour and show excellent attention to detail. With a cosy library area, and large windows looking out onto the garden, this is a chic oasis of calm in the city centre, where you can easily while away hours over dinner.

€€

—

Via Conca del Naviglio 37, 20123 Milano
acasaeatery.it
+39 02 36743350

Alice

In 2014, a new branch of the produce superstore Eataly (pg. 39) opened in Milan's Teatre Smeraldo. The complex includes cafés and bars, and on the top floor you will find the Michelin-starred restaurant Alice, which has been in operation for ten years under the direction of chef Viviana Varese and maître d' and sommelier Sandra Ciciriello. The interiors are bright, warm and elegant, with lots of white and oak, dashes of greenery, and large windows offering views of the square below. The menu is Mediterranean in style (the fish dishes are particularly good) and the wine list is vast and varied. For a special occasion you can chose the 'Viviana' or 'Sandrina' tasting menus. Advance booking is strongly advised. Closed on Sundays.

€€€€

—

Piazza 25 Aprile 10, 20121 Milano
aliceristorante.it
+39 02 49497340

Bacaro del Sambuco

This tiny restaurant is a hidden gem in Milan's high-end shopping area. Just opposite Dior and under an archway, it is a charming family-run business that attracts a very well-to-do clientele of businesspeople and luxury shoppers. If you can, get a table in the courtyard (heaters and blankets are provided in crisper weather) and enjoy a long, delicious lunch of fresh seafood, silky pasta dishes and moreish desserts. The owners (the mother is the chef, the father runs front-of-house, and their daughter is a waitress and sometime-interpreter) are beyond accommodating, and their passion for their food and their business is clear in every dish. Open for lunch only, 9.30am to 6pm, Monday to Saturday. Booking is advised.

€€€

—

Via Monte Napoleone 13, 20121 Milano
ilsambuco.it
+39 02 76394832

Carlo e Camilla in Segheria

Located in the Navigli area, Carlo e Camilla can be difficult to find, and you'd be forgiven for thinking you're in the wrong place when you see the unassuming exterior of this 1930s sawmill. However, a magical experience awaits you inside. The space is the brainchild of art director Tanja Solci (whose grandparents once owned the mill) and Michelin-starred chef Carlo Cracco, and with manager Nicola Fanti they have created something very special. The décor is cool and industrial, with two long banquet tables lit by vintage chandeliers, and the dishes and cocktails are works of art. Simultaneously raw and refined, Carlo e Camilla is a unique restaurant and cocktail bar, where every element has been carefully considered to celebrate quality and design.

€€€

—

Via Giuseppe Meda 24, 20141 Milano
carloecamillainsegheria.it
+39 02 8373963

Ceresio 7

Ceresio 7, the brainchild of DSquared2 designers Dean and Dan Caten, is a stunning rooftop bar and restaurant atop the fashion house's headquarters. The complex includes a bar, a restaurant and two long swimming pools where you can unwind during the day and enjoy the magnificent views (entry to the pool is €110 per person). The excellent restaurant is run by Elio Sironi, formerly of the Bulgari Hotel, and his menu is a heady mix of luxurious ingredients and classic Italian dishes. The décor is as bold and fashionable as you could expect of the Catens, with sharp lines and prints by Basquiat on the walls. The service is slick and the atmosphere is electric, so, for the fashion set, Ceresio 7 is the place to see and be seen.

€€€€

—

Via Ceresio 7, 20154 Milano
ceresio7.com
+39 02 31039221

Giacomo

€€€

This old school bistrot is decidedly masculine in style, with shelves of leather-bound books, dark wood and rich red fabrics, and the whole experience of dining at Giacomo is aptly elegant and classic. It is open for lunch and dinner seven days a week, but it is at its best in the evening, when it is frequented by aristocrats, fashionistas and business leaders. The menu is heavy with beef, game, rich seafood and truffles, but vegetarians are also well catered for. The wine list is expertly curated, and the martinis are second to none. A French throwback with English touches in downtown Milan, Giacomo is a warm, tasteful and buzzing place to spend a relaxing, memorable evening.

—

Via Pasquale Sottocorno 6, 20129 Milano
giacomobistrot.com
+39 02 76022653

L'Arab-esque

€€€

L'Arabesque is a cult interiors, fashion and book store that was opened by designer and collector Chichi Meroni in 2010 to bring together tailor-made clothing and vintage fashion, accessories and furniture from the 1920s to the 1960s. The mid-century theme is continued into the restaurant, with its 1950s furniture, mismatched lightshades and antique Chinese prints. It is open every day from 7.30am to 11pm, serving breakfast, lunch and dinner, and the menus take their inspiration from Meroni's 1999 recipe book, *Once Upon a Time at Table*. Meroni is a fascinating creative powerhouse who has curated this sprawling oasis on her own terms; the restaurant, with its focus on high-quality modern takes on classic dishes, is the perfect representation of her philosophy.

—

Largo Augusto 10, 20122 Milano
larabesque.net
+39 02 76014825

Larte

Larte is an innovative restaurant, a stone's throw from La Scala, that brings food, fashion, art, design and business together under one stylish roof. Inspired by Altagamma, which is a foundation that introduces top-level Italian brands for collaboration and development, Larte contains a restaurant, a café, a chocolate shop, and an art gallery, encapsulating all that is great about Italian life, presented to the highest standards. It's unsurprising, then, that this is one of the most popular locations for business lunches in Milan. There is a focus on regional ingredients and cooking processes, and in addition, all of the sleek décor is available to buy. Larte is open for breakfast, lunch and dinner, and booking is advised.

€€€€

—

Via A. Manzoni 5, 20121 Milano
lartemilano.com
+39 02 89096950

Drogheria Milanese

Part restaurant, part deli, Dogheria Milanese is a wonderful
marriage of traditional Italian cooking and modern social dining.
On entering Drogheria 'Carobbio', you're met with the smell of
truffles, and the space and staff are immediately welcoming.
The décor is bright and airy, with a slim central communal table,
separate tables for larger groups, and bar seating. The menu
features classic dishes and small plates, and the emphasis is on
using the best ingredients with a light touch. We recommend you
select a number of small plates to enjoy the quality of the produce
on offer, and that you leave room for one of the excellent classic
desserts. The friendly service and bustling atmosphere makes
this a lively place to meet friends for lunch, dinner or an aperitivo.

€

Via Conca del Naviglio 7, 20123 Milano; Drogheria 'San Marco', Via San Marco 29, 20121 Milano
drogheriamilanese.com
+39 02 58114843; +39 02 45488837

Olmetto

Chic young restaurant Olmetto opened in late 2015, but the building it inhabits, the Palazzo Brivio Sforza, is over six centuries old; this heritage is evident in the impressive wine cellar, but otherwise the atmosphere is cool and modern, with eclectic mid-twentieth-century furniture and rich jewel tones. The kitchen is supervised by Michelin-starred legends Pia Buonamici and Remigio Berton, who guide the younger chefs in the quest to refine traditional Italian cuisine with a focus on the best possible ingredients. The chefs are particularly proud of their Catalan lobster and paccheri alla Genovese, but customers often return for the risotto. A favourite with locals, Olmetto's cosy, elegant atmosphere makes it great for large or small groups. The restaurant closes for three weeks every August, so check the website in advance.

€€

—

Via Disciplini 20, 20123 Milano
ristoranteolmetto.it
+39 02 91663899

Pacifico

Situated on the corner of Via San Marco and Via della Moscova, Restaurant Pacifico specialises in Peruvian haute cuisine. Chef Jaime Pesaque is regarded as one of the best in the world, and in just two years he has established this restaurant as one of Milan's finest. It is divided into a Pisco Bar, a private lounge, and the main restaurant, and the interiors are dark and sexy, with lots of blue velvet and marble. The food is fascinating; Peruvian cuisine is tinged with Asian and European influences, and here it is finely tuned. We recommend you begin with a signature Pisco Sour cocktail, and be sure to sample the ceviche, which is spectacular. A favourite with locals and visitors, Pacifico grows lively into the evening, making it the perfect place for a chic dinner and drinks.

€€€

Via della Moscova 29, 20121 Milano
wearepacifico.it
+39 02 87244737

Risoelatte

A few steps from the Plaza del Duomo, Risoelatte is a unique restaurant that will transport you back to 1960s Italy. Over three floors of apparent organised chaos, the owners have recreated a lively retro home; all of the plates and glassware date from the period and a vintage Wurlitzer provides the perfect soundtrack. Undergarments hang from the mezzanine as if to dry, and the bathroom is complete with old-fashioned curlers and shaving foam. But that is not to say that style is prized over substance: the menu is concise and it is updated monthly, according to the ingredients of the season, and all bread, pasta and desserts are homemade. The quality of the food and the character of the space makes Risoelatte a memorable and intimate dining experience.

€€

—

Via Manfredo Camperio 6, 20123 Milano
risoelatte.com
+39 02 39831040

A Santa Lucia

A Santa Lucia was opened in Via Agnello in 1929 by Modena native Leone Legnani, and his Neapolitan cooking quickly made the restaurant a firm favourite with celebrity clientele of stage and screen. The restaurant moved to its current location in 1957, but the association with notable diners continued (Frank Sinatra, Maria Callas and Liza Minnellli are among the customer portraits on the walls). The menu has also retained its old-world charm, and the waiting staff are happy to recommend from the list of fresh pizzas, *al dente* pastas, hearty meats and robust Italian wines. Extremely popular with locals, A Santa Lucia is a restaurant that is rightfully proud of its heritage and position as a Milanese institution.

€€€

—

Via S. Pietro all'Orto 3, 20121 Milano
asantalucia.it
+39 02 76023155

T'a Milano

T'a Milano is the ideal city centre haven at any time of the day or night. It is owned by Tancredi and Alberto Alemagna, whose family are synonymous with Italian baking and confectionery. Gioacchino Alemagna established Milan's first luxury bakeries after the First World War, and now Tancredi and Alberto have brought the family trade into the twenty-first century with T'a Milano, a beautiful art deco bistro with an adjoining chocolaterie and patisserie selling all manner of sweet delicacies. The room was designed by renowned architect Vincenzo De Cotiis, and against a backdrop of rich blues, veined marble and huge windows, guests can enjoy coffees, breakfast, lunch, dinner or cocktails, before buying some of the famous artisan chocolates to take home.

€€€

—

Via Clerici 1, 20121 Milano
tamilano.com
+39 02 87386130

The Small

When Milanese handbag designer Giancarlo Petriglia set out to open a restaurant, he knew that he wanted to create a unique dining experience, and while the Small is indeed tiny, it packs a powerful punch. As a result, these are intimate and highly sought-after tables. The charming owner's personality is writ large in the interiors, which are packed with artworks and unusual vintage pieces. While the space shows that the Small doesn't take itself too seriously, the food is extremely well-crafted cuisine and the menu is frequently updated according to the season. It is no wonder, then, that the restaurant attracts a very cool clientele. Advance booking is essential.

€€€€

—

Via Niccolò Paganini 3, 20131 Milano
thesmall.it
+39 02 20240943

Antica Trattoria della Pesa

Opened in 1880 in a former weighing station, Antica Trattoria della Pesa is one of the most highly regarded restaurants among the Milanese, and upon entering it is like stepping back into another era. The restaurant prides itself on exquisite traditional cooking, and at lunchtime you can expect to see elegantly dressed customers enjoying traditional dishes such as vitello tonnato, risotto al salto, and osso buco. The space is intimate and lovingly maintained, with crisp linens and fresh flowers. A Milan institution that never fails to impress, Antica Trattoria della Pesa's food, décor and atmosphere are all classic, authentic and refined. It is open for lunch and for dinner (go before 8pm if you don't have a reservation). Closed on Sunday.

€€€

—

Viale Pasubio 10, 20154 Milano
anticatrattoriadellapesa.com
+39 02 6555741

Vasiliki Kouzina

Originally from Greece, Vasiliki Pierrakea worked in marketing in Milan for a number of years before spotting a gap in the market for high-quality, authentic Greek cuisine served in a stylish setting. Vasiliki Kouzina is her reimagining of the typical Greek restaurant, with lush, deep colours and designer furniture, and it has quickly built a strong reputation for delicious food and warm service. The menu is inspired by the proprietor's grandmother's home cooking, and you can expect to find classics such as roast lamb in red wine, taramasalata, and meatballs with courgette and mint on the menu, alongside an intriguing list of Greek wines. Vasiliki's passion for food, style and attention to detail is clear throughout, and Vasiliki Kouzina achieves that delicate balance of cosy and sophisticated. Closed on Tuesday.

€€

—

Via Clusone 6, 20135 Milano
vasilikikouzina.com
+39 02 94381405

Zazà Ramen

If you are craving a break from rich Italian food, independent ramen bar Zazà Ramen is ideal. The interiors, like the flavours, are clean, bright, simple and refreshing, and you can sit at a table or grab a seat at the bar, where you can watch the chefs at work. The ramen broths are infused with shoyu, shio or miso, and are served with pancetta, tofu, beef or octopus. There is also a wide selection of appetisers (including beautiful gyoza), an extensive sake menu, cocktails and artisanal beers. The service is fast and friendly, making this an enjoyable place to take time out from shopping for something healthy and delicious.

€

Via Solferino 48, 20121 Milano
zazaramen.it
+39 02 36799000

Cafés

Emporio Armani Caffè
Bar Luce
Cova
Giacomo Caffè
oTTo

Luini
Pasticceria Cucchi
Marchesi 1824
Sant Ambroeus

Emporio Armani Caffè

Armani is a name that needs no introduction, and this *caffè* is part of the fashion house's impressive building on the high-end shopping street via Manzoni. The décor is as slick as you would expect, and the food is similarly well presented. There is wide menu on offer throughout the day; try the risotto, and stay for an Aperol Spritz and some people-watching. Don't let the luxury name put you off – the menu is well priced and the crowd is a blend of tourists, local shoppers and associates having informal business meetings (the dress code veers towards smart casual). Perfect for a long lunch or a quick break from shopping, this café is a chic and casual way to experience the world of Armani.

Via Croce Rossa 2, 20121 Milano
armanirestaurants.com/milano-emporio-armani-caffe
+39 02 72318680

Bar Luce

The film director Wes Anderson was tasked with creating
the bar in the OMA-designed Prada Foundation (pg. 52), and
he clearly relished the challenge. Like his films, the concept
is highly stylised and full of pastel colours, and could not
have been conceived by anyone but Anderson. The space is
inspired by Milanese cafés from the 1950s and '60s, and uses
references from famous Milanese landmarks; the patterned
wallpaper above the bar, for example, is inspired by the
Galleria Vittorio Emanuele II. Kitsch details such as veneered
wooden panelling on the walls, upholstered Formica furniture,
jukeboxes and Steve Zissou-themed pinball machines make
this an incredibly fun place to have a drink.

—

Largo Isarco 2, 20139 Milano
fondazioneprada.org/barluce/
+39 02 56662611

Cova

Cova is more than a café, it is a symbol of Milan's recent history and future direction. It was opened by veteran Antonio Cova in 1817, on the corner of Piazza della Scala, and became a favourite haunt of the upper classes and literati. It survived the First World War (it is namechecked in Hemingway's *A Farewell to Arms*), then the Second, and in 1950 it was relocated to via Montenapoleone, which was soon to become the city's important luxury shopping district. The elegant interior, service and cuisine remained prized for decades, and in 2013, Cova's position as Milan's premium café was reinforced when it was acquired by LVMH, who plan to operate the café and bring its particular brand of sophistication to new cities around the world.

—

Via Montenapoleone 8, 20121 Milano
covamilano.com
+39 02 76005599

Giacomo Caffè

This classic café, just steps from the Duomo and the Royal Palace, is a part of the influential Giacomo group, which includes Giacomo Restaurant (pg. 68). The atmosphere here is one of old-world elegance, and it is delightfully quiet, considering its prime location. Stop for a homemade pastry with your breakfast coffee, or one of their classic Italian dishes at lunchtime, and do your best to get a table upstairs. It's an ideal location for an apertivo as well, and the friendly staff will serve you complimentary snacks with your drinks. We recommend the Nobo, a Bloody Mary with whiskey instead of vodka.

—

Piazza Duomo 12, 20121 Milano
giacomomilano.com
+39 02 89096698

oTTo

oTTo has a distinctly minimal Nordic aesthetic, with a muted palette, re-covered chairs and stools, and potted plants adorning the walls. Located in Sarpi, Milan's Chinatown, it has a cool, laid-back atmosphere, and you'll notice many of the young customers using their laptops while they sip on coffees. It serves breakfast, lunch and dinner, stays open late, and the terrace is the perfect spot in fine weather.

—

Via Paolo Sarpi 8, 20154 Milano
sarpiotto.com
+39 02 83417249

Luini

Luini is a famous spot among tourists and locals. Down a small street off Corso Vittorio Emanuele II, you might spot a queue forming outside around lunchtime. Since 1888, people have been flocking to this Milanese institution to purchase one of their superb panzerotti – a traditional street food from Puglia, made of pizza dough and stuffed with tomato and mozzarella. It's more of a kiosk than a café, so the panzerotti come wrapped in paper and are eaten on the go. Definitely worth the wait.

—

Via Santa Radegonda 16, 20121 Milano
luini.it
+39 02 86461917

Pasticceria Cucchi

Pasticceria Cucchi is a great place to come for a drink if you want to step back into the spirit of Milan in the *dolce vita* years. Established in 1936 and rebuilt following the Second World War, this family-run business has an old-world charm, with waiters in formal attire and décor from the 1950s. From morning to evening it is full of stylish Milanese people, sipping on espresso and enjoying aperitivi. Make sure to sample one of their famous cakes or pastries while you're there.

—

Corso Genova 1, 20123 Milano
pasticceriacucchi.it
+39 02 89409793

Marchesi
1824

If you're looking for a stylish pit stop to revive your spirits during a day's shopping, head straight for this relatively new branch of Pasticceria Marchesi. Founded in 1824, Pasticceria Marchesi has expanded in recent years, thanks to its acquisition by the Prada Group, and now there are three locations: in this luxury shopping arcade, at via Monte Napoleone 9, and at via Santa Maria alla Porta 11/a (where you will find the historic pastry shop that opened in 1824). Join the impeccably dressed crowd to enjoy finger sandwiches, champagne, cakes and cocktails amidst the quite beautiful chartreuse and pastel interiors, and look down through the arched windows at the people rushing across the mosaics of the mall below.

—

Galleria Vittorio Emanuele II, 20121 Milano
pasticceriamarchesi.com
+39 02 94181710

Sant Ambroeus

Opened in 1936, Sant Ambroeus is the height of Milanese elegance. Despite its location in the centre of the shopping district, it is very much a café for city dwellers, who bustle along the bar, espressos in hand, catching up with one another. The staff always extend a warm welcome to tourists as well, of course, so come for a pastry and a top-rate cappuccino, or have a classic Italian lunch in the restaurant. The décor is elegant and understated, save for the stunning Murano chandelier that shimmers over the dining room. Very centrally located just a few steps from La Scala, Sant Ambroeus offers the quintessential café experience in Milan, and is the perfect way to begin or end a day in the city.

—

Corso Matteotti 7, 20121 Milano
santambroeusmilano.it
+39 02 40042266

Bars & Clubs

Bar Basso

Bar Basso is credited with democratising the concept of the aperitivo in Milan, which had previously been the reserve of exclusive international hotel bars. It opened in 1947, and has been serving high-quality cocktails to a devoted clientele ever since. Today it draws cocktail connoisseurs and design aficionados, who come to enjoy its old-world glamour and vast list of over 500 drinks. Bar Basso has achieved the difficult task of maintaining its classic nineteenth-century style and Milanese heritage, and winning new fans from all over the world, year after year. No visit to Milan would be complete without savouring Bar Basso's signature Negroni Sbagliato; made with prosecco instead of gin, it is served in a huge glass with a giant hand-cut ice cube.

—

Via Plinio 39, 20020 Milano
barbasso.com
+39 02 29400580

Bicerìn

That the proprietors of Bicerìn love and respect Italy's relationship with wine can be in no doubt. The environment in this hidden gem of a wine bar has been carefully considered to create a warm and relaxing atmosphere, where it is as comfortable to read a book with a glass of wine as it is to chat with friends over several. More than 800 wines and sherries are represented, which you can enjoy by the glass or bottle, and there is a concise menu of savoury and sweet dishes available, including cured meats, cheeses and Cantabrian anchovies that are perfect for sharing. Bicerìn is open every day from 6.30pm to midnight, and reserving a table in advance is advisable.

—

Via Panfilo Castaldi 24, 20124 Milano
bicerinmilano.com
+39 02 84258410

The Botanical Club

The Botanical Club is a must for lovers of gin: established in 2015, it is a cocktail bar, bistro, and the first small-batch gin distillery in Milan. Their gin is called Spleen et Idéal ('Flowers of Evil'), and each batch they produce is named after a girl. There is also a huge selection of international gins, a gin and tonic menu that changes every month, and a tempting and affordable cocktail list. The food menu offers a great range of punchy small plates, such as crunchy octopus or mushroom 'cappuccino', alongside classic Italian and French main dishes. The premises in the Isola neighbourhood was soon followed by another in Via Tortona in the Navigli, which transposes the cool aesthetic of the original onto a larger scale.

—

Via Pastrengo 11, 20159 Milano
thebotanicalclub.com
+39 02 36523846

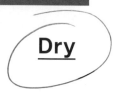

Dry

Dry, the name a wry nod towards the speakeasies of the Prohibition, is the work of creative collective 'food.different', who also run the very successful Pisacco in the city, and this second venture is the group's interpretation of the 'DRY principle' in software engineering: Don't Repeat Yourself. Everything is stripped back to its essential ingredients: the décor is stark and edgy (the specials are written on the bare walls), the pizzas are inexpensive and delicious, and the cocktails are pure science, with every drink on the vintage-inspired list made with modern precision. The music is excellent, and the art director hand-picks video art pieces that are projected onto the walls, reinforcing the feeling that there is nothing ordinary about Dry.

—

Via Solferino 33, 20124 Milano
drymilano.it
+39 02 63793414

Fonderie Milanesi

Those who take the time to find Fonderie Milanesi will be rewarded with a buzzing atmosphere and a taste of old rustic Italy. Situated off the beaten track, between Porta Romana and Porta Genova, you must cross a number of courtyards before arriving at a gate, where a bell will grant you entry to the old foundry building. Fonderie Milanesi offers a unique marriage of traditional and hipster Milan. Brunch and dinner are served, but it is best at aperitivo time, when the cocktails flow and the crowd swells. It is open Tuesday to Sunday, and gets very busy as the evening progresses, so we recommend that you go early; arriving by 7pm should give you a choice of great seats.

—

Via Giovenale 7, 20136 Milano
fonderiemilanesi.it
+39 02 36527913

Mag Cafè

Mag Cafè is another stand-out bar in the popular Navigli district, serving some of the area's best cocktails in a cool, sexy setting. The bar is owned by Flavio Angiolillo and Marco Russo, who have taken particular care of crafting the interior, including importing the antique furniture from the original Mag pharmacy in Argentina. Coffees, snacks, and standard drinks are sold all day; take a seat on the terrace by the canal first, then go inside to watch the bartenders at their mesmerising work when they begin serving the cocktail menu at 5.30pm. Next door, Angiolillo and Russo have another trick up their sleeves; Backdoor43, an exclusive 4 square metre bar where you can order drinks through a hatch to enjoy *al fresco*.

—

Ripa di Porta Ticinese 43, 20143 Milano
+39 02 39562875

Officina Cocktail Bar

Officina is an open-air cocktail bar that began life as a pop-up in via Giovenale 7, a cool, out-of-the-way courtyard that has become a popular haunt for young creatives. The concept of the pop-up was a cocktail workshop in collaboration with Officine Riunite Milanesi, a real motorcycle repair and customisation company. This blend of muscular motorbikes and delicate cocktails sounds unusual, but with the mixologists using modern techniques (including smoking processes, nitrogen, and transformative blocks of ice), it was a huge hit and the collaboration was made permanent. The aesthetic is appropriately sparse and unpretentious; strings of plain lightbulbs span the courtyard, illuminating vintage garage touches, and making this a chilled place to unwind with a drink and to watch the evening kick into gear.

—

Via Giovenale 7, 20136 Milano
officineriunitemilanesi.it
+39 333 2139112

<u>Ugo</u>

Located on a street thronged with drinking emporiums, Ugo refers to itself as 'the Unusual Bar', and it does indeed stand out, with its beautiful décor, intimate ambience and exquisite service. The atmosphere is great throughout the week, and the crowd is a nice mix of locals and young, cool tourists. The cocktails are reasonably priced and crafted with extreme care, and there is also an affordable food menu that includes bruschettas, burgers, and light meals. The Navigli district has a great deal to offer in the evening, so we recommend that you head straight to Ugo for a cocktail and snack, before taking a stroll to explore the area.

—

Via Corsico 12, 20144 Milano
ugobar.it
+39 02 39811557

Check
What's
On

Blue Note Milano

Blue Note Milano is a jazz club and part of the Blue Note Network, which has its origins in the famous Blue Note of Greenwich Village, New York, but now has locations in Japan, China, Slovakia, and Italy. The Milan premises opened in 2003, and the bar has live music performances every evening except Mondays, totalling around 350 shows per year. Check the website for listings before you go, and when you book you can select the option to enjoy dinner during the show. The kitchen serves refined Italian and classic international dishes, and alongside good Italian and French wines there are over 200 cocktails to choose from. With excellent music and a distinguished environment, the Blue Note offers a grown-up evening of entertainment.

—

Via Pietro Borsieri 37, 20159 Milano
bluenotemilano.com
+39 02 69016888

Fabrique

Fabrique is a live music, DJ and club venue located in the centre of the fashion district. It was founded by Daniel Orland, a young businessman from Milan who saw the potential for an exciting new event space, and he chose to situate it in a warehouse that was once home to Venus Discs, famed music distributors. With a capacity of around 3,000, the space has been expertly designed to ensure the best sound quality and views of the stage. The bar staff are courteous and quick, and there is a nice outdoor area for smokers. Expect to see performers like Fatboy Slim, Massive Attack and Arcade Fire on the diverse programme.

—

Via Gaudenzio Fantoli 9, 20138
fabriquemilano.it
+39 02 58018197

Hangar Bicocca

HangarBicocca is a remarkable not-for-profit contemporary art space housed in the buildings of a former Pirelli factory. It is one of Europe's largest exhibition spaces, covering 15,000 square metres. This is focused on three buildings, Shed, Navate, and Cubo, the original features of which have been preserved and play a role in the exhibition experience. HangarBicocca opened in 2012, and has already hosted some of the world's most important artists. On permanent exhibit is Anselm Kiefer's singular 'Seven Heavenly Palaces 2004-2015', which was commissioned specially for the opening of the venue. Exhibitions are open from 10am to 10pm, and admission is free, but the space is occasionally closed to the public for special events, so check the website before you visit.

—

Via Chiese 2, 20126 Milano
hangarbicocca.org
+39 02 66111573

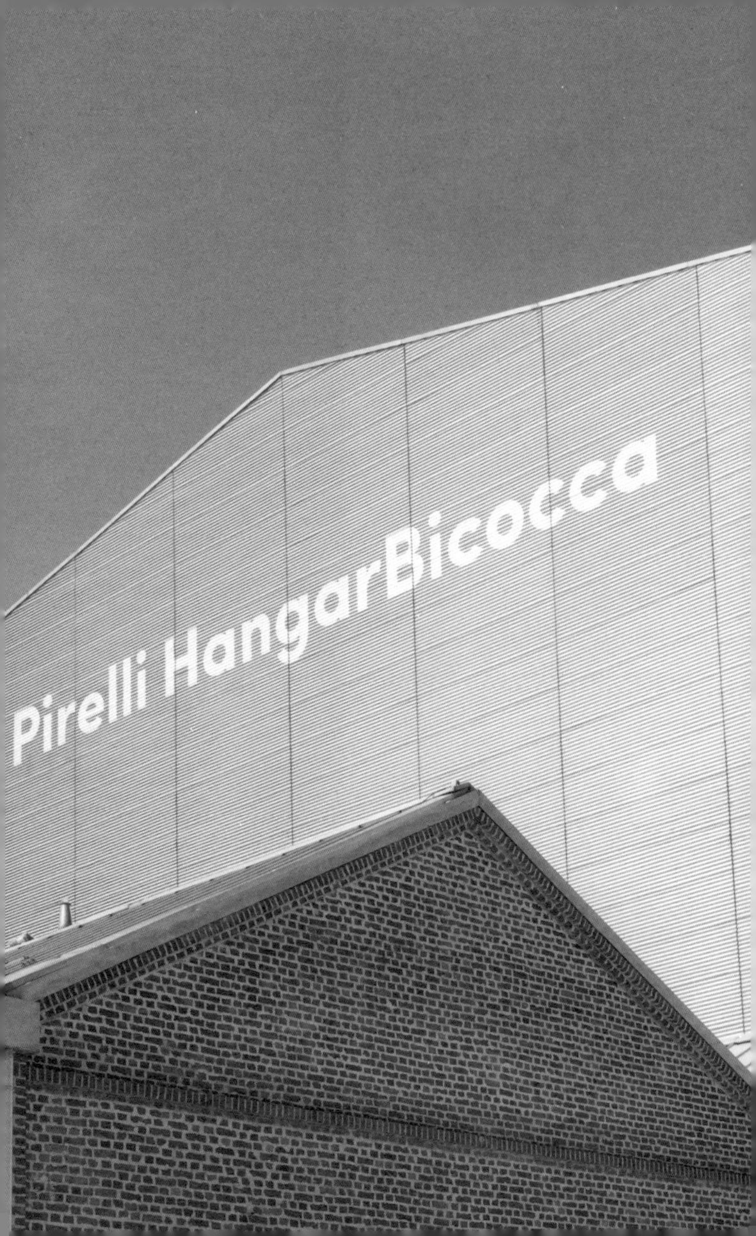
Pirelli HangarBicocca

Palazzo
Reale

The fourteenth-century Palazzo Reale, perfectly located on Piazza del Duomo, is one of Milan's most impressive and popular cultural spaces. It was built by the Visconti family, and updated in the sixteenth-century by the Sforzas. It suffered extensive damage during World War II, and full restoration is still ongoing. Here, visitors can view world-class permanent and temporary exhibitions, featuring artists such as Bacon, Kandinsky, Hiroshige, Rubens and Escher. Admission to the palace is €12 per adult, and temporary exhibitions cost an additional €12-€20. Galleries are quieter on weekdays, and you can beat the queues every day by buying an advance ticket online. Palazzo Reale will delight art lovers, and its opulent setting and careful, informative curation will appeal to everyone.

—

Piazza del Duomo 12, 20122 Milano
palazzorealemilano.it
+39 02 88465230

Teatro alla Scala

For over two centuries elegantly dressed crowds have gathered here to watch the best operatic artists and ballet performers from Italy and beyond, and Teatro alla Scala remains one of the best-regarded theatres in the world. Ticket prices vary significantly (a ticket to *Madama Butterfly*, for example, can cost anywhere between €15 and €250) but if you go to the box office two hours before a show commences, a number of last-minute tickets go on sale (one hour before the show, remaining tickets, if any, are sold at a 25 per cent discount). If you don't have time to attend a performance, the Theatre Museum has a collection of art and artefacts that celebrates all the history and glamour of Teatro alla Scala.

—

Via Filodrammatici 2, 20121 Milano
teatroallascala.org
+39 02 88791

Before you visit Milan, you might want to check out these books and films to give you a better sense of the city.

Books

Accidental Death of an Anarchist
Dario Fo

Dario Fo's Nobel prize-winning *Accidental Death of an Anarchist* is an absurd drama based on real-life events in 1969, when an anarchist railwayman, a suspect in the Piazza Fontana bombing, fell to his death from a fourth-floor window of a Milan police station. The play is a fictionalised version events that comments on political corruption, capitalism and the government in a supremely witty and enjoyable way.

The Betrothed
Alessandro Manzoni

First published in 1827, *The Betrothed* is widely regarded as one of the most important Italian novels ever written. Set in the 1620s in Lombardy,

then occupied by the Spanish, it is the epic story of two lovers, Renzo and Lucia, as they battle to overcome separation, oppression and plague. A timeless rumination on love, power and humanity, it is also lauded for its evocative descriptions of Milan and its environs during that period.

A Farewell to Arms
Ernest Hemingway

A Farewell to Arms is Hemingway's classic semi-autobiographical novel that follows a love story that unfolds against the backdrop of the First World War in Italy. American Frederic Henry is serving as a lieutenant in the ambulance corps of the Italian Army (as the author had done) when he meets English nurse Catherine Barkley; their romance is

plagued with numerous difficulties, and they both find themselves in Milan. However, their trials do not end there. A moving story, written with Hemingway's characteristic direct tone and understated precision.

Foucault's Pendulum
Umberto Eco

Foucault's Pendulum is definitely not light reading but your perseverence will be rewarded. The novel is richly detailed, dense with references and requires a certain amount of knowledge about conspiracy theories, history, religion, alchemy, and Freemasonry. In the story, three Milanese editors start to work on 'The Plan', which is a fictional intellectual game based on conspiracy theories. After a while they realise that fiction and reality are all mixed up.

Films

I am Love
2009

'When I moved to Italy, I learned to be Italian,' says Tilda Swinton in *I Am Love*, and we have no choice but to trust her. She is as stunning as usual as Emma, an elegant Russian-born woman who moved to Milan because of her husband, and became part of a bourgeois, powerful industrial family. Even though her life seems perfect, Emma feels unfulfilled. What could happen next? A dish of seafood and ratatouille, dim lights and a handsome chef changes everything.

Valentino: The Last Emperor
2008

If you are fond of fashion, then this gem of a movie is for you. It lies somewhere between a documentary and a biopic, as it charts a year in the life of the legendary haute couturier Valentino Garavani as he prepares his 2006 Spring/Summer collection. Alongside the processes and sheer workload involved in preparing a collection at this level, the film gives an insight into the genius's personal life and character, as well as his influential relationship with Giancarlo Giammetti, and the glamorous world of high fashion.

Vincere
2009

Vincere is a grim, dark historical drama about Ida Dasler, Benito Mussolini's secret lover. She fell in love with the Fascist leader around 1910 and gave birth to a boy, Benito Albino. After the outbreak of World War I they lost touch, and they only met again years later in a hospital, when Ida discovered Mussolini's other wife and daughter. This absorbing dusky movie reveals the private life of the dictator from another, unknown point of view.

What Scoundrels Men Are!
1932

If you can, seek out this wonderful vintage romantic comedy. It tells the story of Bruno, played by Vittorio De Sica (who would go on to become one of Italy's most influential directors), a chauffeur who uses his car to pretend to be rich and important in order to impress a girl. They head off on an adventure around the city and into the country, but as you might expect, the ruse does not play out smoothly. In a move quite unheard of at the time, the film was shot on location around the city, making it a unique document of Milanese life in the 1930s.

Check out these sites and accounts for the most up-do-date events and insights into life in Milan:

Influencers

The Blonde Salad
theblondesalad.com

Founded by Milan locals Chiara Ferragni and Riccardo Pozzoli, this style blog has grown into one of the most popular in the world.

Camera Moda
cameramoda.it

Camera Nazionale della Moda Italiana is the top authority on Milan fashion news and events.

Conosco Un Posto
aplaceinmilan.com

An attractive guide to food, culture, and the Milan lifestyle.

Elena Ciprietti
@elenaciprietti

A New Yorker based in Milan, Ciprietti's Instagram shows a terrific eye for Milan's interesting details.

The Fashion Fruit
thefashionfruit.com

Milan-based Veronica Ferror and her partner Giorgio Merlin started The Fashion Fruit in 2010, and it quickly became one of Italy's top fashion blogs.

Mi mag
mimag.it

An English-language web magazine focused on the culture, entertainment, and style of Milan.

Pasquale Ieluzzi
@linoieluzziofficial

Pasquale 'Lino' Ieluzzi is the owner of haberdashery Al Basar di Lino Ieluzzi and a *bone fide* Milan style icon.

Rossana Orlandi
@rossana_orlandi

For the latest finds by Milan's *grand dame* of design (pg. 48).

Where Milan
wheremilan.com

For the latest news and events in Milan.

The Whisper Society
thewhispersociety.com

Tess Harwood's beautiful vintage-tinged guide to Milan's hidden gems.

Tips from the inside: we asked some top Milan creatives for their favourite spots

Contributors

Carlo Cracco
@carlocracco

Carlo Cracco is an internationally celebrated chef and a towering figure in Italian cuisine. Having worked in a number of award-winning restaurants, in 2007 he opened Restaurant Cracco in Milan, which has since received two Michelin stars and been ranked among the top fifty restaurants in the world. Cracco is also a household name thanks to his television work.

'My favourite restaurant in Milan is Wicky's Wicuisine Seafood (wicuisine.it/) on Corso Italia. It specialises in Kaiseki cuisine and combines Japanese techniques and Mediterranean ingredients. Afterwards I might head to Carlo e Camilla in Segheria (pg.65).

'You should visit Fondazione Prada (pg. 52), of course, but also the church of San Maurizio al Monastero Maggiore, a beautiful early sixteenth-century edifice on Corso Magenta. If you are interested in cuisine, go to my favourite shop, Coltelleria Lorenzi (o-lorenzi.it/). It is an iconic knife shop that has been in business for almost a century. '

Irene Crocco
viasaterna.com

Irene Crocco is a curator and founder of Viasaterna, a contemporary art gallery set over two levels in a beautiful late-nineteenth-century building on Via Leopardi. The gallery opened in 2015 and quickly established itself as an important hub for exhibitions and events.

'My favourite institution in Milan (besides our gallery Viasaterna, of course!) is Fondazione Prada, especially their new venue Osservatorio, which is in Galleria Vittorio Emanuele II (fondazioneprada.org/visit/milano-osservatorio).

'All the artists that have exhibited in Viasaterna have raved about the nearby local restaurant L'infinito (ristoranteinfinito.com). It's a traditional restaurant that has never changed; they serve classic, simple Italian cuisine in a familiar, cosy atmosphere. Another great place to eat is Maio (maiorestaurant.com) on top of La Rinascente (pg. 43), which offers one of the closest views of the Duomo.

'I recommend a visit to the Santa Maria presso San Satiro (Via Torino, 17/19). It is one of the oldest churches in Milan, and it was designed by the great architect Donato Bramante. The interior, in particular, is amazing.

'To shop, I like Wait and See (pg. 49) for its creative accessories and clothes, and Massimo Alba (massimoalba.com), whose collections are usually classic and innovative at the same time, with lots of colour and fun designs.'

DIMORESTUDIO
dimorestudio.eu

Designers Emiliano Salci and Britt Moran founded DIMORESTUDIO in 2003, and the practice encompasses art, design, fashion and architecture. Described by Forbes magazine as 'the Prada of the design world', the studio is one of the most influential in Europe and is in high demand with fashion houses and hotels. Among their stunning projects is Ceresio 7 (pg. 66).

'To dine, we recommend La Latteria San Marco (Via S. Marco, 24), an iconic little restaurant, run by husband and wife, Arturo and Maria, who serve simple meals of superior quality. It's extremely popular and does not accept reservations, but it's worth doing what you can to get a table. Also good are A Santa Lucia (pg. 79) and Trattoria Torre di Pisa (trattoriatorredipisa.it).

'For the evening try Fioraio Bianchi (fioraiobianchicaffe.it). This elegant Parisian-style café has been in business for over forty years, and is always full of fresh flowers. Plastic (facebook.com/plasticmilano) is great for dancing and people-watching, and stays open until 5am.'

Federico Poletti
@fedepoletti

Federico Poletti is a well-known journalist and independent fashion curator. Co-founder and Editor-in-Chief of manintown.com, he has written for Huffington Post Italy, D la Repubblica, Vogue and Vanity Fair Italia. He has also written several books, including The Fashion Set: The Art of the Fashion Show, and Crafting the Future, with Franca Sozzani.

'My favourite restaurant is The Small (pg. 82), which is an arty destination with typical Italian cooking with a focus on Mediterranean land- and seafood. It was conceived by the bag designer Giancarlo Petriglia, and it has a fairy-tale atmosphere, thanks to the surreal design objects, art pieces and decorations spread all over the place.

'Bar Basso (pg. 102) describes the very essence of the Milan of today and yesteryear. It's attended by artists, designers, creative people, and those loving good drinks. You can choose from a list of 500 cocktails, but the most famous are the historic Rossini or Negroni Sbagliato, which is the authentic Milanese aperitivo.

'Hidden from the hustle and bustle of Milan's city centre, Nonostante Marras (antoniomarras.com) is a store and a meeting place that hosts a variety of cultural events. It is the brainchild of Patrizia Marras, the wife of the Italian designer Antonio Marras. Here you might find books, clothes, objets retrouvés, pictures, old chairs, or even catch a few fragments of a poem, all in a relaxed, soft, embracing atmosphere.

'Wok (wok-store.com) is a concept store focused on a blend of emerging labels and more widely known brands. It offers a good balance of edgy and avant-garde style from all over the world, and fashion also meets art here through dedicated events and exhibitions.

'Finally, Fondazione Prada (pg. 52) is a must, and especially Bar Luce (pg. 89), which was designed by Wes Anderson. In taking inspiration from Italian pop culture of the 1950s and '60s, he has created a real movie set for the cafè of the Prada Foundation.'

Leonardo Scotti
leonardoscotti.com

Leonardo Scotti is a freelance photographer, born and raised in Milan. Upon graduating he worked as photo assistant to Pierpaolo Ferrari, with whom he continues to collaborate on projects like Toilet Paper Magazine, *and he also works in fashion, advertising and print. Recent clients include Burberry, JW Anderson, Missoni,* Vogue, *and* Wallpaper*.

'My favourite restaurant is Al Garghet (algarghet.it); it is a true Milanese restaurant – really elegant and traditional. There's an old man playing piano, a handwritten menu in Milanese dialect, and they serve the best cotoletta [veal breaded cutlet] in the city. It's a little out of the centre, so book a couple of days before to secure a table.

'In Milan there is a big difference between bars and clubs: bars must close at 2am, and after that you go to the club. I like easy bars with a relaxed mood, and I often go to Colorificio in Via Cesariano (facebook.com/colorificiocesariano) which is a small and cosy place located in a great pedestrian area close to other bars and restaurants. My favourite club in Milan is not really a club, as such; it's an itinerant party that changes place almost every month. It's called DOGS (facebook.com/DO.G.S.Milan) and it has become very big in the last few years.

'For shopping I like to go to Humana (humanavintage.it), which is a vintage store connected to an international charity that works to improve life in the world's poorest countries. If you're lucky you can find some really amazing stuff, and you're also helping people around the world. The best place for art in Milan is Hangar Bicocca (pg. 124). It brings the best artists from all over the world – and it's free! You can reach it with the new purple line of the subway.

'In terms of other amazing places, you must see the Cimitero Monumentale di Milano (the Monumental Cemetery, Piazzale Cimitero Monumentale) - believe me!'

Photography Credits

Pg. 6, Conor Clinch, Pg.8 Getty Images/Simone Simone, Pg.13 Straf Hotel, Pg.14 Palazzo Segreti, Pg.16 3 Corso Como, Pg.18 Armani Hotel, Pg.19 Armani Hotel, Pg.20 Madama Hostel, Pg.21 Madama Hostel, Pg.22 Palazzo Segreti, Pg.23 Palazzo Segreti, Pg.24 Room Mate Giulia, Pg.25 Room Mate Giulia, Pg.26 Senato Hotel, Robert Holden, Pg.28 Straf Hotel, Barbara Santoro, Pg.29 Straf Hotel, Barbara Santoro, Pg.30 The Yard, Pg.31 The Yard, Pg.32 10 Corso Como, Pg.34 10 Corso Como, Pg.35 10 Corso Como, Pg.36 Antonia, Pg.37 Antonia, Pg.38 Biffi, Solange Souza, Pg.39 Eataly, Pg.40 Excelsior Milano, Pg.42 Frip, Pg.43 Getty ImagesStefania D'Alessandro/Stringer, Pg.44 Nilufar, Mattia Iotti, Pg.45 Nilufar, Mattia Iotti, Pg.46 Peck, Pg.48 Spazio Rossana Orlandi, Pg.49 Wait and See, Pg.50 Patricia Gimeno, Pg.52 Riccardo Bianchini/Alamy Stock Photo, Pg.54 Getty Images/AFP/Staff, Pg.55 guillermohor/Shutterstock.com, Pg.56 Paolo Bona/Shutterstock.com, Pg.58 Foto di arenaimmagini.it, 2014 © FAI - Fondo Ambiente Italiano, Pg.59 Foto di arenaimmagini.it, 2014 © FAI - Fondo Ambiente Italiano, Pg.60 Olmetto, Jule Hering, Pg.62 A Casa Eatery, Cristina Gualmini, Pg.63 Alice, Pg.64 Bacaro del Sambuco, Pg.65 Carlo e Camilla, Chico de Luigi, Pg.66 Ceresio 7, Pg.67 Ceresio 7, Pg.68 Giacomo, Massimo Listr, Pg.70 L'Arabesque, Yorick Photohgraphy, Pg.72 Larte, Pg.73 Drogheria , Pg.74 Olmetto, Jule Hering, Pg.75 Olmetto, Jule Hering, Pg.76 Pacifico, Zeno Zotti, Pg.77 Pacifico, Zeno Zotti, Pg.78 Riseolatte, Pg.79 A Santa Lucia, Merih Yurtkuran, Pg.80 T'a Milano, Federica Santeusanio/matteovolta.com, Pg.81 T'a Milano, Federica Santeusanio/matteovolta.com, Pg.82 The Small, Michele Mancano, Pg.83 Aurora Photos/Alamy Stock Photo, Pg.84 Vasiliki Kouzina, Federico Villa, Pg.85 Zaza Ramen, Pg.86 Giacomo Café, Cristina Galliena, Pg.88 Emporio Armani Caffe, Pg.89 Bar Luce, Fondazione Prada, Pg.90 Getty Images/Giuseppe Cacace/Staff, Pg.91 Giacomo, Ivan Lattuada, Pg.92 Da oTto, Pg.94 MARKA/Alamy Stock Photo, Pg.95 Pasticceria Cucchi, Pg.96 Pasticceria Marchesi, Agostino Osio, Pg.98 Getty Images/Mondadori Portfolio/Contributor, Pg.100 Giacomo Arengario, Massimo Listri, Pg.102 Bar Basso, Pg.103 Bicerin, Helenio Barbetta, Pg.104 The Botanical Club, Saverio Lonmbardi Valluari, Pg.105 The Botanical Club, Pg.106 Dry, Pg.108 Fonderie Milanesi, Paulina Arcklin, Pg.109 Fonderie Milanesi, Paulina Arcklin, Pg.110 Mag Café, Tess Harwood, The Whisper Society, Pg.111 Officina, Tess Harwood, The Whisper Society, Pg.112 Ugo, Pg.113 Ugo, Pg.114 Patricia Gimeno, Pg.116 Bailey-Cooper Photography/Alamy Stock Photo, Pg.117 Alessio Orru/Shutterstock.com, Pg.118 pierdea/Shutterstock.com, Pg.120 Patricia Gimeno, Pg.122 Blue Note, Pg.123 Getty Images/Mondadori Portfolio/Contributor, Pg.124 Hangar Bicocca, Lorenzo Palmieri, Pg.126 Getty Images/Bloomberg/Contributor, Pg.128 Teatro alla Scala, Brescia/Amisano, Pg.129 Teatro alla Scala, Brescia/Amisano, Pg.130 pcruciatti/Shutterstock.com